LITTLE BLACK BOOK

DAILY MOTIVATION FOR BUSINESS & PERSONAL GROWTH

LOUIS CARR

Copyright © 2016 by Louis Carr

All rights reserved. No part of this book may be reproduced or transmitted in any form by any means, electric or mechanical, including photocopying, recording, or by any information storage and retrieval system without permission in writing from the publisher, except by a reviewer, who may quote brief passages in a review.

Published by Seraph Books, LLC
www.seraphbooks.com

www.LouisCarrBook.com
www.LouisCarrFoundation.org

ISBN: 978-1-941711-19-4
Library of Congress Control Number: 2016937706

PRINTED AND BOUND IN THE UNITED STATES OF AMERICA
10 9 8 7 6 5 4 3 2 1

Cover design by Alyssa M. Curry

Copyediting by Alyssa M. Curry

Author photo by Akintayo Adewole for
Adewole Photography, www.adewole.com

For information regarding special discounts for bulk purchases of this book for educational, gift purposes, as a charitable donation, or to arrange a speaking event, please visit: www.seraphbooks.com

LITTLE BLACK BOOK

INTRODUCTION

THERE WILL be occasions when you need motivation in your personal and professional life. It is necessary to acquire knowledge that is sustaining and can help you push through the challenges you may be facing when trying to reach your goals. Consequently, there will be moments when you need faith, maturity, or comprehension.

This *Little Black Book: Daily Motivation for Business & Personal Growth* is a companion to my memoir, *Dirty Little Secrets*. In it, I share some advice and secrets that are beneficial to one's overall growth. You will know when and where these lessons are applicable—and remember to share them!

"All in, all the time" means you are committed to a goal, vision, or plan *all of the time*.

LOUIS CARR

> Take an account of the reality by obtaining an understanding of what happened, how the situation happened, and why.

Just as there is sunshine, there is rain; and I look at God's Word as an umbrella that is going to protect me.

LOUIS CARR

Your journey will test you.
Make sure to learn from your
trials, blessings, and miracles
because they will happen.

Knowledge gives you the basic
things you need for vision.

If you do not have vision,
you had better hope you run
into a vision maker.

LITTLE BLACK BOOK

Allow others to participate
in your vision or dream.

LOUIS CARR

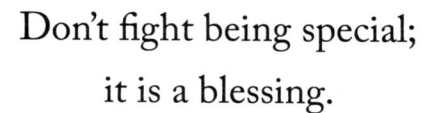

Don't fight being special;
it is a blessing.

Some people do not know what
hard work is. They think it is
about time spent. It is
not about the time, it is
about the intensity.

LOUIS CARR

Do not be afraid to operate in an uncomfortable space; it is only going to help you grow.

When you commit to making a transition to something new, take time to prepare appropriately. Never underestimate the difficulty of change.

Being in an uncomfortable place is the way to set goals, have vision, and stretch yourself beyond what you have ever done or think you can do.

Ego should not be the thing
that holds us back from
the greatness God has
set us here for.

LOUIS CARR

You can take risks. Just make sure they are calculated risks.

Some people can display an out-of-control ego but when their head hits the pillow at night, they know the real deal.

Once you reach the point where you dislike the rules that are established, become a game changer and you can make different decisions.

To reinvent yourself, you have
to expand your boundaries
of information and
communication.

Being able to reinvent yourself
is the key for anyone
who wants to grow.

You should care about your image because it always extends beyond you.

LOUIS CARR

When you think of your image, understand that it is not just physical; it is mental, emotional, and about your preparedness.

In life, you set the tempo.
You determine how fast you
want to go by your willingness
to put in the work.

LOUIS CARR

If you do not have discipline,
you are like a leaf blowing
down the street. You will
end up anywhere.

Most successful people
have a vision that is
bigger than themselves.

LOUIS CARR

Leadership is exhibited by
using your will, skill,
and influence for the
benefit of others.

Great leaders should be
able to see around the corner.

At the end of the day, great teams have their members on the same page all the time.

The way to achieve consistency
is through practice. You see
it in business, and in sports.
It is evident in the environment,
and the outcome will be
reflected in the results.

Train yourself to be a solution-oriented person, but be cognizant of the timeline.

There is a myth that the higher you go, the easier it is. It is the exact opposite. The higher you go, the greater the responsibility.

LOUIS CARR

Get to know your children. Understand where they are coming from and then shape and guide them along the way.

Set expectations, have consistency, and make sure your children understand you care.

LOUIS CARR

Faith is hard because we do not
know when answers or solutions
are going to come but the
key is, they will come.

Every situation we find ourselves in is a growth opportunity. It does not matter if it is negative or positive; it is what you choose to make of it.

Let's not forget what God did for us two weeks ago, last year, or five years ago. Since life is constantly moving, we have the tendency to forget.

When it comes to having a successful marriage, those core values and beliefs act like conductors that facilitate a stronger connection.

LOUIS CARR

In a marriage, the journey is not just for one, it is for both people.

If your company and your vision are not looking like what America or the world looks like, you have a lot of work to do.

Bringing a diverse group of
people together will take
your management skills
to the next level.

Prepare your environment
and yourself by expanding
your boundaries.

The process of maturity will help you begin to see yourself with an honest deliberation regarding your actions.

There is always something you have to overcome in order to have some type of maturity.

People who are still in the
growth process will
apologize for their behavior
without justification.

Miracles happen because they are part of a person's predestination.

Excuses and old rules will
hold you back; so learn
how to win by new rules.

Sometimes the faith test can
be a minute and sometimes it
can seem like a lifetime.

LOUIS CARR

It takes more energy to catch up than to keep up.

There is one thing that hasn't changed in the history of the world—and that is Jesus.

LOUIS CARR

Especially in difficult times, remind yourself that you believe what you believe.

Since life is moving constantly, you can forget what God has done for you. You may start to think it was your actions that got you out of that situation.

Change and growth are an inevitable part of your journey.

You cannot achieve your vision without reinventing yourself along the way. You have to learn new things.

LOUIS CARR

Learn to push through
and attack anything that is
difficult physically, mentally, or
emotionally. Do not run away
from it. Meet it head-on.

Hard work is only going to get you so far in business. Physical, mental, and emotional skills are needed to take you to the next level.

LOUIS CARR

Know what it is like to prepare.
Understand that some of your
free time isn't free.

Every situation is a growth situation regardless if it is negative or positive. The determining factor is what you choose to make of it.

You cannot have envy or jealousy. If someone has more than you and you want it, determine how to go to work and get yours, not theirs.

Understand how big the opportunity is and try to make it bigger for more people to enter.

Your purpose is a journey. Along that journey there are going to be a lot of things you are supposed to do, there is not one particular thing. You have to take the journey in order to know what the end looks like.

You will know what maturity feels like when you are able to control your emotions.

LOUIS CARR

It is not a journey unless you can measure it. If you cannot measure it, you are in the same place.

In order to have vision you must come out of that comfortable place.

Preparation puts the foundation in place, which allows you to work on the things that are essential to your success.

Success is a lifestyle; not in the traditional way but as it pertains to behavior. Do the work.

Joy killers are not happy for
your success because they
operate to kill your joy;
so use them as motivators.

When it comes to business,
you are measured by the
results, not feelings.

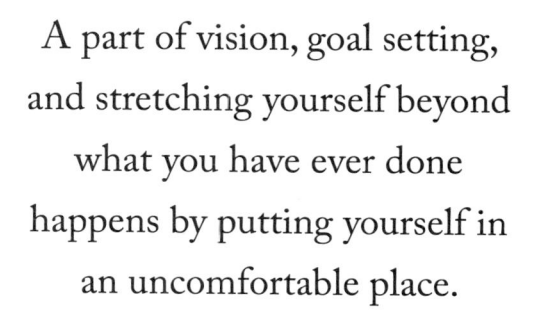

A part of vision, goal setting, and stretching yourself beyond what you have ever done happens by putting yourself in an uncomfortable place.

In order to be successful, you must first believe it is for you.

Allow everything you do to
focus around being successful.

Take the initiative to do things
that expand your capacity
beyond what you think it is.

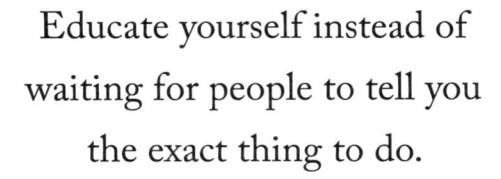

Educate yourself instead of waiting for people to tell you the exact thing to do.

Sometimes the growth is emotional, nutritional, physical, and mental. All are necessary throughout your journey.

LOUIS CARR

Challenges can help you grow.

Vision can be created for you
until you see it for yourself.

Some people are without the understanding of possibilities. When they see a door close, they do not see another one open. That closed door may be what is needed to see a greater opportunity.

LITTLE BLACK BOOK

Leadership is visual.

LOUIS CARR

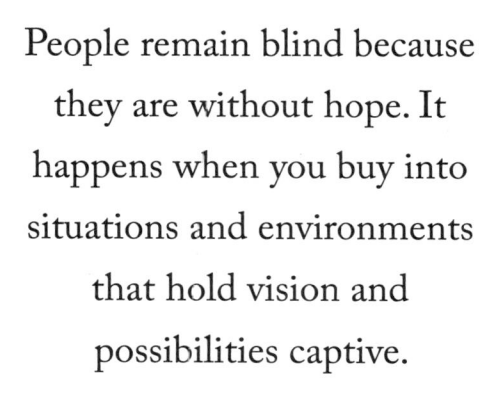

People remain blind because they are without hope. It happens when you buy into situations and environments that hold vision and possibilities captive.

Every situation, every environment, everyplace, and everything is temporary. Nothing lasts a lifetime.

Things change every day and they will either be negative or positive changes. The decision as to how you view these changes is your choice.

When you do not understand
change is constant,
you limit your possibilities.

There are a lot of participants in a stadium. There are fans, cheerleaders, players, coaches, security personnel, owners, and more. The decision is yours as to which uniform you are going to wear and that will depend on how you believe you can make a difference.

Always inspect what you expect.

When someone pours vision into you, you will not know if it is right for you until you try it. That is what is exciting about life.

LITTLE BLACK BOOK

To be great,
just see the greatest in God.

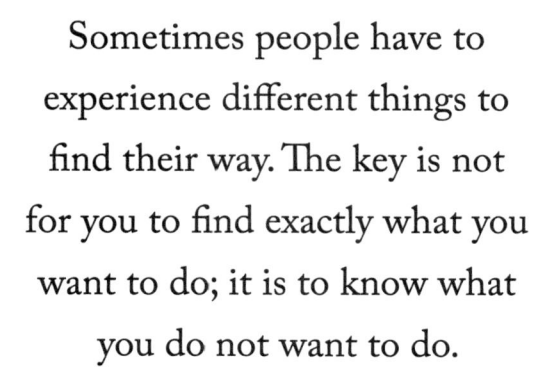

Sometimes people have to experience different things to find their way. The key is not for you to find exactly what you want to do; it is to know what you do not want to do.

Your greatest battles in life
will be with yourself,
not with someone else.

LOUIS CARR

Even when you are tired, you have to force yourself to do it. At the end of the day, you are not preparing yourself for the good times, you are preparing yourself for the bad times.

When you find yourself with a lack of understanding and there is confusion in your life—that is when you need faith.

Life is one continuous preparation for your journey. If you are not prepared for the journey or do not understand you are on a journey, life is going to be difficult.

If you work toward making others great you will realize the greatness in yourself.

LOUIS CARR

There are four directions: backward, forward, right, and left. If you are going right and left you are going side to side and you may not be going forward but you may be running in place at that moment in time. The thing you do not want to do is go backward.

You cannot grow without
a journey. It is
absolutely necessary.

LOUIS CARR

Make your goals
bigger than yourself.

If you are managing people
from diverse backgrounds,
you must adopt and engage
a management style that will
motivate all of them toward
setting goals, achieving results,
and meeting expectations based
on what motivates them.

LOUIS CARR

Be as mentally tough as
you are physically tough.

Great managers, like great coaches, use the things they need to get the best out of people. You must understand what motivates, influences, and inspires each person to be the best that they can be.

LOUIS CARR

The importance of a journey
is that it exposes you to
a great deal.

Successful managers have multiple management styles to get the best out of people. You cannot motivate, inspire, or lead people unless you understand them.

LOUIS CARR

If you get to know a person
a little more than average,
they will know you care.

Try to be transparent with your team so there are no surprises.

When you are tested, the
length of time depends on your
faith. The greater your faith,
the shorter the test.

In order to lead people,
you should be a
subject-matter expert.

LOUIS CARR

One of the mistakes we make, that could help us recover faster, is we tend not to use our past faith experiences to get us through.

People who do not have patience have forgotten how much they did not know.

Realize you are on a journey, and just because things do not work out now, does not mean they will not work out next week, next month, or next year.

Put enough work in to
believe you deserve to win.

Just because things are well
now, does not mean you do not
have to prepare yourself for
when things are bad.

Use every workout as a step toward the winner's circle.

By nature, we are a selfish people. The value of serving people is the lesson that is necessary to end selfishness.

To be a great manager, don't
be so concerned about yourself,
be concerned about those
who work for you.

LOUIS CARR

Life owes you nothing—and yet, gives you the opportunity to have anything.

ABOUT THE AUTHOR

LOUIS CARR, President of Black Entertainment Television Media Sales, is one of the most influential and prominent African Americans in the media and marketing industries. He has been responsible for more advertising dollars targeted toward the African-American consumer market than any other professional or company. He

ABOUT THE AUTHOR

has been listed on NAMIC's Most Influential African Americans in the cable industry several times and received the Legend Award from Ad Color in 2013.

He has served on the boards of the Ad Council; International Radio and Television Society (IRTS); American Advertising Federation (AAF); and the Video Advertising Board (VAB), formerly the CAB.

He is a dedicated mentor and benevolent philanthropist. An advocate for diversity, Mr. Carr has hired more people of color and has the most diverse sales team than any other executive or company in the media industry. For more than twelve years, the Louis Carr Internship Foundation has dedicated its efforts to improve diversity in corporate America.

He currently serves on the board of the Boys Hope Girls Hope and the United States Track and Field Foundation. Mr. Carr resides in Chicago, Illinois, with his wife, Diane.

www.LouisCarrBook.com

www.LouisCarrFoundation.org